How to Analyze the Works of

SUZANNE
COLLINS

by Sheila Llanas

ABDO
Publishing Company

How to Analyze the Works of

SUZANNE
COLLINS

by Sheila Llanas

Content Consultant: Joseph J. Foy, Assistant Professor
Department of Political Science, Law, and Philosophy
University of Wisconsin-Parkside

Credits

Published by ABDO Publishing Company, PO Box 398166, Minneapolis, MN 55439. Copyright © 2013 by Abdo Consulting Group, Inc. International copyrights reserved in all countries. No part of this book may be reproduced in any form without written permission from the publisher. The Essential Library™ is a trademark and logo of ABDO Publishing Company.

Printed in the United States of America,
North Mankato, Minnesota
042012
092012

 THIS BOOK CONTAINS AT LEAST 10% RECYCLED MATERIALS.

Editor: Lauren Coss
Series Designer: Marie Tupy

Library of Congress Cataloging-in-Publication Data
Llanas, Sheila Griffin, 1958-
  How to analyze the works of Suzanne Collins / Sheila Llanas.
    p. cm. -- (Essential critiques)
  Includes bibliographical references.
  ISBN 978-1-61783-456-1
  1. Collins, Suzanne--Criticism and interpretation--Juvenile literature. I. Title.
  PS3603.O4558
  813'.6--dc23
                                        2012013118

Table of Contents

Chapter

1

Introduction to Critiques

What Is Critical Theory?

What do you usually do when you read a book? You probably absorb the specific language style of the book. You learn about the characters as they are developed through thoughts, dialogue, and other interactions. You may like or dislike a character more than others. You might be drawn in by the plot of the book, eager to find out what happens at the end. Yet these are only a few of many possible ways of understanding and appreciating a book. What if you are interested in delving more deeply? You might want to learn more about the author and how his or her personal background is reflected in the book. Or you might want to examine what the book says about society—how it depicts the roles of

women and minorities, for example. If so, you have entered the realm of critical theory.

Critical theory helps you learn how various works of art, literature, music, theater, film, and other endeavors either support or challenge the way society behaves. Critical theory is the evaluation and interpretation of a work using different philosophies, or schools of thought. Critical theory can be used to understand all types of cultural productions.

There are many different critical theories. If you are analyzing literature, each theory asks you to look at the work from a different perspective. Some theories address social issues, while others focus on the writer's life or the time period in which the book was written or set. For example, the critical theory that asks how an author's life affected the work is called biographical criticism. Other common schools of criticism include historical criticism, feminist criticism, psychological criticism, and New Criticism, which examines a work solely within the context of the work itself.

What Is the Purpose of Critical Theory?

Critical theory can open your mind to new ways of thinking. It can help you evaluate a book from a new perspective, directing your attention to issues and messages you may not otherwise recognize in a work. For example, applying feminist criticism to a book may make you aware of female stereotypes perpetuated in the work. Applying a critical theory to a book helps you learn about the person who created it or the society that enjoyed it. You can also explore how the work is perceived by current cultures.

How Do You Apply Critical Theory?

You conduct a critique when you use a critical theory to examine and question a work. The theory you choose is a lens through which you can view the work, or a springboard for asking questions about the work. Applying a critical theory helps you think critically about the work. You are free to question the work and make an assertion about it. If you choose to examine a book using biographical theory, for example, you want to know how the author's personal background or education inspired or shaped the work. You could explore why the author was drawn to the story. For instance, are there any parallels between a particular character's life and the author's life?

Forming a Thesis

Ask your question and find answers in the work or other related materials. Then you can create a thesis. The thesis is the key point in your critique. It is your argument about the work based on the tenets, or beliefs, of the theory you are using. For example, if you are using biographical theory to ask how the author's life inspired the work, your thesis could be worded as follows: Writer Teng Xiong, raised in refugee camps in

> ### How to Make a Thesis Statement
>
> In a critique, a thesis statement typically appears at the end of the introductory paragraph. It is usually only one sentence long and states the author's main idea.

Southeast Asia, drew upon her experiences to write
the novel *No Home for Me*.

Providing Evidence

Once you have formed a thesis, you must
provide evidence to support it. Evidence might
take the form of examples and quotations from the
work itself—such as dialogue from a character.
Articles about the book or personal interviews with
the author might also support your ideas. You may
wish to address what other critics have written
about the work. Quotes from these individuals may
help support your claim. If you
find any quotes or examples that
contradict your thesis, you will
need to create an argument against
them. For instance: Many critics
have pointed to the protagonist of
No Home for Me as a powerless
victim of circumstances. However,
in the chapter "My Destiny," she is
clearly depicted as someone who
seeks to shape her own future.

How to Support
a Thesis Statement

A critique should include
several arguments. Arguments
support a thesis claim.
An argument is one or
two sentences long and is
supported by evidence from
the work being discussed.

Organize the arguments
into paragraphs. These
paragraphs make up the
body of the critique.

In This Book

In this book, you will read summaries of the books of the Hunger Games series by writer Suzanne Collins, each followed by a critique. Each critique will use one theory and apply it to one work. Critical thinking sections will give you a chance to consider other theses and questions about the work. Did you agree with the author's application of the theory? What other questions are raised by the thesis and its arguments? You can also find out what other critics think about each particular book. Then, in the You Critique It section in the final pages of this book, you will have an opportunity to create your own critique.

Look for the Guides

Throughout the chapters that analyze the works, thesis statements have been highlighted. The box next to the thesis helps explain what questions are being raised about the work. Supporting arguments have been underlined. The boxes next to the arguments help explain how these points support the thesis. Look for these guides throughout each critique.

Suzanne Collins wrote the best-selling trilogy The Hunger Games.

2

A Closer Look at Suzanne Collins

Suzanne Collins was born in Connecticut in 1962 to Michael and Jane Collins. She had three older siblings, Kathy, Joanie, and Drew. Because her father was a military man, the Collins family moved a lot, living on or near military bases in the United States and Europe. As a child, Suzanne watched cadets at West Point Military Academy in New York practice on the field.

A Military Upbringing

In 1968, when Suzanne was six years old, her family moved to Indiana. That same year, her father began a yearlong tour of duty in Vietnam, fighting in the Vietnam War (1954–1975). Jane tried to prevent her children from seeing the graphic images of the war on television and in the newspapers.

Sometimes, however, Suzanne saw these images by accident. She knew her father fought in the violent war shown on television. It frightened her to think of her father in such a dangerous place. She missed him greatly during the years he was gone. "If your parent is deployed and you are that young, you spend the whole time wondering where they are and waiting for them to come home," she later said in an interview for the *New York Times* magazine.[1]

When Michael came home from Vietnam a year later, he suffered extreme anxiety resulting from intensely traumatic experiences. Anxiety disorders, such as post-traumatic stress disorder (PTSD), are common among soldiers returning from war. For the rest of his life, Michael had nightmares. Sometimes Suzanne woke at night when her father cried out in his sleep.

Lessons from Books and War

As a young girl, Suzanne loved to read. From her mother, she learned to love Greek mythology and science fiction. Suzanne loved reading books from these genres. At age eight, she read the myth of Theseus and the Minotaur. Her favorite novels included *A Wrinkle in Time* by Madeleine L'Engle and *The Phantom Tollbooth* by Norton Juster and Jules Feiffer. She also loved *A Tree Grows in Brooklyn* by Betty Smith and *1984* by George Orwell. Suzanne read these novels over and over. In fifth and sixth grade, her English teacher read gruesome tales by Edgar Allan Poe aloud to the class. Suzanne recalls being riveted. Poe's stories made a big impression on her.

After returning from Vietnam, Michael pursued a career in the Air Force. He was also a highly educated military historian with a doctorate degree in political science. He taught at military schools and colleges around the country, and he held positions with NATO and the Pentagon. Each new position for her father meant a move for Suzanne and her family.

When Suzanne was in seventh grade, around 1974, her family moved to Brussels, Belgium, where Michael was stationed. The Collins family lived in Belgium for the next four years, and Suzanne began studying at an American school there in seventh grade. While they were in Europe, Michael took Suzanne on tours of historic sites, including battlefields. Michael was a good storyteller and knew how to talk about historical events in ways that made them into gripping stories. He lectured his children in graphic detail about battles, weapons, and military strategy. It was important to him to educate his children about war. When Suzanne was in tenth grade, the family moved back to the United States.

A Career in Television

After graduating high school from the Alabama School of Fine Arts in 1980, Collins studied at Indiana University, where she majored in both theater and telecommunications. She also met her future husband, Cap Pryor, who was an actor. When the couple moved to New York City, she earned her master of fine arts degree in dramatic writing at New York University.

In 1991, Collins began working in children's television. She wrote for children's cartoon shows including *Wow! Wow! Wubbzy!* and *Clifford's Puppy Days*. She also worked on shows geared toward young adults, such as *Clarissa Explains it All* and *The Mystery Files of Shelby Woo*.

Collins and her husband eventually had two children, Charlie and Isabel. They moved from New York City to Connecticut for more space. By 2001, Collins had a lot of experience in children's writing.

Collins wrote for the popular 1990s show *Clarissa Explains It All*, starring actress Melissa Joan Hart.

While working on a children's show for the Warner Brothers network, Collins met children's author James Proimos. Proimos believed she had the mind of a novelist and suggested she write a book.

Down a Manhole: Collins's First Book

With Proimos's encouragement, Collins began her first novel, *Gregor the Overlander*. The premise was loosely based on the novel *Alice in Wonderland* by Lewis Carroll. Collins changed the natural setting of the original story to an urban environment. The main character, Gregor, falls down a dark New York City basement vent and lands in the Underworld, a place filled with giant rats, bats, cockroaches, and other city creatures. She applied the same principles to writing novels that she followed to write cartoon scripts for children's television. Though descriptive passages were new to her, the dialogue came easily. Because she was used to writing condensed scripts, Collins knew how to heighten tension in fast-paced, high-action plots. Her cliff-hanger chapter endings kept readers riveted. "Whatever age you're writing for," she later said, "the same rules of plot, character, and theme apply."[2]

Gregor the Overlander features war themes and battle scenes. For advice on writing about war, Collins turned to an expert—her father. She and Michael spent hours discussing military strategies, war weapons, and military alliances. Her father would never see the outcome of these discussions in print; he died before the book was published. Scholastic published *Gregor the Overlander* in 2003, when Collins was 41 years old.

Gregor the Overlander was the first book in the Underland Chronicles, a five-book series geared toward middle-grade readers. The books, which were published one per year until 2007, feature biological warfare, genocide, death, and loss— tough themes for kids. But Collins believes pre-teens and teenagers can handle tough themes. "If it's filled with cuddly animated animals, chances are no one's going to die," she said. "If it's filled with giant flesh-and-blood rats with a grudge, there's going to be violence."[3] She was the same age as many of her readers when her teacher read Edgar Allan Poe stories and her father taught her about war.

Inspiration Strikes: The Idea for the Hunger Games

One night before going to sleep, Collins lay in bed watching television. She flipped back and forth between a reality television program and coverage of the wars in Iraq and Afghanistan. On one channel, a group of people competed for a prize. On the other channel, soldiers outfitted in full combat gear fought a real war. The lines between the two media stories began to blur in Collins's mind.

Inspired by the potential of such a combination, Collins set out to create Panem, a futuristic dystopia which would become the setting for the Hunger Games series. In a 2010 interview, Collins discussed the importance of dystopian stories:

> *Dystopian stories are places where you can play out the scenarios in your head—your anxieties—and see what might come of them. And, hopefully, as a young person, with the possibilities of the future waiting for you, you're thinking about how to head these things off.*[4]

The Structure of the Hunger Games

Collins wanted to write the Hunger Games series for a teenage audience, an older audience than that of the Underland Chronicles. To adapt to older readers, Collins stripped out elements of fantasy, such as talking animals, and increased the levels of violence.

Collins knew the Hunger Games series would be a trilogy, a structure she had grown comfortable with as a playwright and screenwriter. Before writing, Collins set out the major plot points for each of the three books, such as the inciting incident, crisis, and climax. Each book has 27 chapters, broken into three sections of nine chapters each. She gave each book a different core plot.

Because Collins knew she was creating a trilogy, the books are closely linked. The writing of the three Hunger Games books merged when Collins revised the first book while writing the second book. "Since each book feeds into the next," she said during that time, "I feel like part of my brain's been in Panem continuously."[5] Collins did her homework while writing. While researching protagonist Katniss Everdeen's primary strengths, her survival skills, Collins read a stack of survival books.

Launched into Fame

Scholastic initially printed 200,000 copies of the first book, titled *The Hunger Games*. The book was released in September 2008, and it became an immediate sensation. When the second book in the trilogy, *Catching Fire*, was released in September 2009, readers were ready. The highly anticipated book quickly became a best seller on lists across the United States. As soon as *Catching Fire* was released, excitement began growing for the third and final installment in the series. Scholastic released no advance copies of the third book and did not send any books out early to reviewers, as is normally done with new books. The press and fans could only speculate what the final book would be like. However, 1.2 million copies were printed in anticipation of the book following the success of the previous two Hunger Games books. When *Mockingjay* launched on August 24, 2010, bookstores held midnight release parties for eager fans. The book was as popular as the publisher and press expected. By this time, the series had even become popular among adult readers.

Collins was now a famous author. As of 2012, the Hunger Games series had been on the New York Times best-seller list for more than three years running. Despite her newfound fame, Collins tries to keep her personal life private. She avoids the camera and rarely allows her interviews or public readings to be captured on film.

From Page to Screen

Because every installment of the Hunger Games series reached the top of best-seller lists, it was not long before the books began generating talk of film adaptations. Lionsgate Entertainment acquired the movie rights to the series in March 2009, before

Catching Fire and *Mockingjay* were even released. Collins wrote the first draft of *The Hunger Games* screenplay. To plan for the movie, Collins spent time in Los Angeles, California. She discussed cast, sets, costumes, and script changes with director Gary Ross. The much-talked-about *Hunger Games* movie was released in March 2012, with a *Catching Fire* film scheduled for release in November 2013.

Director Gary Ross worked closely with Collins to create *The Hunger Games* screenplay.

As of 2012, Collins was working on a semi-autobiographical children's book based on the year her father served in Vietnam. She planned to continue reaching into her past to discover new stories to tell to her eager readers.

Jennifer Lawrence stars as Katniss in the 2012 film adaptation of *The Hunger Games*.

3

An Overview of
The Hunger Games

The Hunger Games takes place in the postapocalyptic dystopian country Panem. The country is divided into 12 districts, which serve a Capitol governed by President Coriolanus Snow and the Peacekeepers, military forces that maintain police control. Capitol residents enjoy excess and privilege, while district citizens struggle in poverty.

Part I: The Tributes

In the early morning, 16-year-old Katniss Everdeen leaves her mother and sister, 12-year-old Primrose, known as Prim, asleep in their small house. The family lives in coal-mining District 12, sometimes called the Seam. Katniss's father was killed in a mining accident five years ago. Ever since, Katniss, a skilled archer like her father, has illegally hunted in the woods outside the district boundaries. In a spot overlooking a valley, she meets her best friend, Gale Hawthorne. They hunt and gather food they will trade at the Hob, the black market in town.

Life is hard for most of the citizens in the 12 districts of Panem. The country once had 13 districts, but District 13 was destroyed after a rebellion almost 75 years in the past. Every year, as punishment for the rebellion, the Capitol holds and televises a brutal Hunger Games in which two children from each remaining district are forced to compete against the representatives from all 12 districts in a televised fight to the death. The last person alive, the victor, is given a lavish home, plus food and money for life. The victor's home district is also rewarded with food and resources.

The lottery to choose tributes, or candidates, for the Hunger Games is known as the reaping. Attendance at the reaping is mandatory, so the townspeople all gather as the names are chosen. The first tribute called is Primrose Everdeen. Katniss immediately volunteers to replace her younger sister as tribute. As she walks to the stage to meet Effie Trinket, District 12's escort from the Capitol, the

people of District 12 offer Katniss an old, silent gesture of admiration and parting.

Next, Effie calls the male tribute's name: Peeta Mellark. Katniss knows Peeta, although she does not

Effie Trinket introduces Katniss as the female tribute for District 12.

think he will remember her. After her father died, when her family was starving, Peeta saved their lives by giving Katniss loaves of burned bread from his family's bakery. Katniss does not want to compete against Peeta because she might have to kill him.

Katniss and Peeta are introduced to Haymitch Abernathy, their mentor who will act as their trainer until the games begin and will be able to provide them with limited aid during the games. Haymitch was a victor from District 12 many years ago, but now he is an alcoholic. Both Katniss and Peeta are frustrated with Haymitch's drunken behavior and poor attitude. Before long, Katniss and Peeta are whisked away on a train to the Capitol.

Once at the Capitol, Katniss meets her stylist, Cinna. Because the lead-up to the Hunger Games and the games are televised, the Capitol wants the tributes to look good. Cinna will design Katniss's costumes and coordinate her appearance during the lead-up to the games. Cinna is the first person Katniss has liked since she arrived at the Capitol.

As tributes from District 12, Katniss and Peeta, are showcased together in the opening ceremonies, their first public appearance. Katniss wears a gold pin her friend Madge from District 12 gave her.

The pin features a mockingjay, a bird evolved from the jabberjay. Jabberjays were birds genetically altered by the Capitol to spy on district citizens. When the Capitol shut down the jabberjay program, the birds were released into the wild where they bred with mockingbirds, creating the mockingjay. The failure of the jabberjays and the mockingjay birds have become an embarrassment to the Capitol.

As Katniss and Peeta ride through the city in a horse-drawn chariot, Katniss's unitard and cape blaze with an artificial fire designed by Cinna. Her costume earns her the label Cinna hoped it would: "the girl who was on fire."[1] The crowd loves her.

Haymitch initially coaches Katniss and Peeta together, but soon Peeta asks to be trained alone. After three days of training the tributes must appear in one final public appearance before the games. Peeta steals the show by announcing to all of Panem that he is in love with Katniss.

Part II: The Games

On the morning of game day, Katniss is lifted into the arena with the other tributes. The Cornucopia, a gigantic horn filled with supplies, is in the center of the arena. The tributes will have to fight over the supplies. When the gong announces the start of the games, Katniss sprints to the Cornucopia and grabs what she can: a backpack and piece of plastic. Even as she races for the woods, the cannon begins firing. Every cannon shot represents a dead tribute. Of the 24 original tributes, 11 have already been killed. When evening comes, Katniss hides herself in the branches of a tree. A screen in the sky shows the faces of the tributes who have been killed that day. To Katniss's relief, Peeta is not among them.

The next day, Katniss gathers food and water. Though she tries to stay hidden from the other tributes, cameras everywhere are recording her every move and televising her actions to all of Panem. Katniss spies a group of career tributes, tributes from the privileged districts who spend much of their lives training for the games. Katniss is shocked to see Peeta working with them.

The next night, as Katniss is in a tree again, a wall of fire speeds toward her spewing fireballs. The Gamemakers, the people in charge of organizing and designing the Hunger Games, have set the fire to create drama. With her leg badly burned, Katniss climbs another tree but the careers discover her hiding spot. They camp beneath her, trapping her in the tree. Rue, another young tribute, is hidden in a nearby tree. She points out to Katniss a deadly hive filled with tracker jackers, a Capitol muttation, or mutt, genetically altered to serve the Capitol. Katniss dumps the tracker jacker hive down on the career tributes, getting stung three times herself with the tracker jackers' poisonous and hallucination-inducing venom. As the careers run to the lake to escape the insects, Katniss lingers to retrieve a bow and arrows left behind. Peeta returns and yells at her to run because the careers are close behind him. Katniss escapes. Just before she falls into a tracker jacker–induced nightmare, she realizes Peeta saved her life with this warning.

After Rue helped her in the tree by pointing out the hive, Katniss decides to form an alliance with Rue. The two devise a plan to destroy the careers' food, stored in the Cornucopia. The next day, Rue lights fires to lure the careers away from the Cornucopia. Katniss discovers the careers have placed mines in the ground around the Cornucopia, so she shoots an arrow into a bag of apples. They spill out, triggering the mines, and the ground explodes. Katniss crawls into hiding just as Cato,

Rue becomes Katniss's ally for a short time during the Hunger Games.

the careers' leader, and the other career tributes return. On her way to reunite with Rue, Katniss arrives to a clearing just in time to see Rue trapped in a net and stabbed by a spear.

Katniss sings to Rue until she dies, then covers her body with flowers—a gesture she knows will infuriate the Capitol. There are now only six tributes left. In an unprecedented move, the games announcer declares the rules have changed. If the last two tributes alive are from the same district, they can both be victors. From her hiding place in a tree, Katniss cries out Peeta's name.

Part III: The Victor

Katniss searches for Peeta and finds him camouflaged so completely into a muddy bank that he is nearly invisible. He is suffering from a bad leg infection. Peeta tells Katniss to act in love with him. He knows the audience likes watching their relationship and will be more likely to send money and gifts. Haymitch will be able to send these gifts, such as food and other resources, directly to Peeta and Katniss. Trying to play along, Katniss kisses Peeta while he is sleeping. In response, Haymitch sends her a pot of hot broth.

Katniss and Peeta are camped in a cave when the games announcer invites tributes to the Cornucopia to collect items they desperately need. For Katniss, this means medicine for Peeta's infection. At the Cornucopia, Katniss faces the remaining tributes, all racing to get their needed items. A boy from Rue's district, Thresh, has the opportunity to kill Katniss, but allows her to escape because of her kindness to Rue. Katniss is able to obtain the medicine for Peeta. Thresh kills one of the career tributes. Five tributes are remaining.

Peeta's leg heals but a deluge of rain forces them to stay in the cave. He and Katniss learn

Thresh is dead. When the weather clears, one of the remaining tributes steals the berries Peeta gathered for himself and Katniss. The tribute instantly dies. Unbeknownst to Peeta, the berries were from the deadly plant nightlock. Katniss saves some berries in her leather pouch.

Now the only tribute left is Cato. Katniss and Peeta are getting water from a lake when they see Cato. He is running away from a pack of mutated wolves. As Katniss fights off the pack with arrows, Cato is overtaken by them. Katniss and Peeta escape from the hounds by hiding on the top of the Cornucopia while the mutated wolves torture Cato. After a long horrendous night, Katniss puts Cato out of his misery with her last arrow. The cannon fires, and Katniss and Peeta believe the games are over.

But nothing happens. Then they hear the announcer's voice. He revokes the new rule that two tributes from the same district could both win. Now only one winner is allowed. Katniss and Peeta refuse to fight each other. Peeta begs Katniss to kill him so she can survive. Suddenly, Katniss knows how to foil the Capitol. She pulls out the poison nightlock berries and gives some to Peeta. He understands they will both eat them and die together. Just before they do, the frantic announcer shouts for them to stop and presents Panem with two victors, a first in the history of the Hunger Games. Katniss and Peeta have both survived the arena.

A hovercraft picks them up and takes them to a Capitol hospital, where they are treated for their injuries. The Gamemakers plan to film the reunion of Katniss and Peeta live. But Haymitch warns Katniss she is still in danger. The Capitol is furious over being made to look foolish. He tells Katniss her defense must be that she was so lovesick she lost her reason. As a victor, Katniss is supposed to be safe for the rest of her life, but during the closing ceremony, President Snow makes it clear he is angry with Katniss. As she endures the interviews and parties immediately following her and Peeta's victory, Katniss fears punishment may arrive at any moment. On the train home, Peeta is dismayed to learn Katniss's love was an act. The train comes to a stop. Finally, she and Peeta have returned to their home in District 12. They take each other's hands one last time for the camera.

As the hero of *The Hunger Games*, Katniss Everdeen exhibits heroic characteristics also found in many other heroes throughout literature.

How to Apply Archetypal Criticism to *The Hunger Games*

What Is Archetypal Criticism?

Archetypal criticism examines cultural and psychological myths in a text. Archetypes are basic, ruling character motifs that express universal experiences. Archetypal criticism is supported by the work of Swiss psychologist Carl Jung, who theorized that all of humanity shares a collective unconscious, memories and desires they are not aware of.

Literary characters have unique individual traits, but they can be interpreted as archetypal if they embody a type of character often seen in other works, such as the wise old sage, the orphan, or the fool. Jung, who said there were countless archetypes, believed archetypal characters represented symbolic truths about the human condition. Archetypal criticism argues that a text's meaning is shaped by cultural and psychological myths. Archetypes give the text meaning. They trigger deeply shared human desires and anxieties. Archetypal images and story patterns encourage readers to participate in the basic beliefs, fears, and anxieties of humanity.

Applying Archetypal Criticism to *The Hunger Games*

Archetypally, *The Hunger Games* represents a literary pattern identified by Joseph Campbell, a scholar of Carl Jung, called the heroic journey. The heroic journey consists of three stages: departure, initiation, and return. In *The Hunger Games*, the hero is 16-year-old Katniss Everdeen. On her journey, she faces many obstacles. In order to conquer external challenges, she has to transform and evolve to fulfill her heroic role. As the archetypal hero of *The Hunger Games*, Katniss evolves from having heroic qualities that support only her family to becoming a hero for all of Panem.

Thesis Statement

The author states the thesis: "As the archetypal hero of *The Hunger Games*, Katniss evolves from having heroic qualities that support only her family to becoming a hero for all of Panem." In this critique, the author traces the evolution of Katniss's heroic tendencies throughout *The Hunger Games*.

As *The Hunger Games* begins, Katniss takes heroic measures to support only her family. Since age 11, she has risked her life by hunting illegally to provide for her mother and Prim. Katniss's heroic efforts have served her well. Her family has survived terrible odds. While the people Katniss defines as family include Gale and his family, Katniss is not overly concerned about her community at large. She sells any leftover food she and Gale have, but she does not gift it to members of her community. Katniss and Gale use the profits from these sales to support their own families.

While Katniss might resent District 12's situation, she does not risk changing it. The townspeople's admiration for Katniss when she steps up to take her sister's place on reaping day suggests those around her recognize her heroism. However, Katniss's only goal in volunteering as tribute is to protect her sister. She is willing to stand by when the Capitol oppresses those around her, but if the Capitol wants to sacrifice her sister, Katniss

Argument One

The author shows the limits of Katniss's heroism with the first argument: "As *The Hunger Games* begins, Katniss takes heroic measures to support only her family."

has no choice but to act. She is not representing Panem or even District 12; her act of self-sacrifice is to protect her family.

As Katniss trains for the Hunger Games, she is troubled by the thought of killing Peeta, even though she has promised Prim she will return. Even though she knows the odds are not in her favor, Katniss is determined to stay alive as long as possible. She has promised Prim she will do whatever it takes to come back to District 12. Prim says to her, "I just want you to come home. You will try, won't you? Really, really try?"[1] Katniss promises she will really, really try. However, Katniss cannot forget Peeta's kindness to her family. They seem to treat each other as allies from the start. They initially agree to be trained by Haymitch together. Then, Katniss is surprised and hurt when Peeta decides to be trained alone. If Katniss's only concern was returning to her sister as promised, she would be able to kill Peeta without a second thought. Instead, she is tormented by the fact

Argument Two

The author's second argument states: "As Katniss trains for the Hunger Games, she is troubled by the thought of killing Peeta, even though she has promised Prim she will return." With this argument, the author shows the gradual shift occurring in Katniss's attitude toward those outside her family.

that in order for either her or Peeta to succeed, the other will have to die. "How do you sidestep that?" she asks.[2] Katniss's heroism does not yet extend to Peeta, but she is troubled by the thought of killing him to save herself and keep her promise to her sister.

Katniss expands her heroism when she stops thinking of her own self-preservation and connects with Rue, the young girl she embraces as an ally. At first, Katniss survives in the arena by keeping a low profile, just as she did in District 12. She slips through the woods, gathering food and analyzing her opponents. She has not designed a proactive strategy yet. When Katniss protects Rue, she becomes proactive for the first time. Katniss forms an offensive plan to destroy the food source of other tributes. She takes charge of her situation. Seeking to protect Rue, Katniss gives herself the most dangerous role in the scheme, leaving Rue the relatively safe task of setting fires. When the plan is enacted, however, Rue is caught in a trap set by another tribute and killed. At this moment, Katniss

> **Argument Three**
>
> The author continues to show Katniss's heroic evolution with the third argument: "Katniss expands her heroism when she stops thinking of her own self-preservation and connects with Rue, the young girl she embraces as an ally."

has an epiphany, realizing, "It's the Capitol I hate, for doing this to all of us."[3] Rue's death forces Katniss to confront the truth. In a gesture she knows will anger the Capitol, she covers Rue's body with flowers. Her goal shifts beyond simply returning to her family as she promised. In this expanded heroic state, she also experiences genuine compassion for Peeta. She now wants to avenge Rue and save Peeta's life. She has undergone a true heroic transformation.

Argument Four

The author's fourth argument states: "After expanding her heroism, Katniss can never return to her old way of being; it is no longer enough to simply protect her family." The author wraps up the arguments by discussing the final stage in Katniss's heroic evolution.

After expanding her heroism, Katniss can never return to her old way of being; it is no longer enough to simply protect her family. Katniss no longer thinks only of herself and her family. She and Peeta are allied when the game rules change to allow two winners. But at the end, when the rule is revoked, Katniss is unable to kill Peeta to save herself, even though he begs her to do so. She is willing to die to foil the true enemy, the Capitol, even though this action will cause Katniss to break her promise to Prim and will likely put her family in danger. She

actually has the poisonous berries in her mouth when the Capitol Gamemakers quickly decide to allow two victors to survive. In an act of heroism that expands beyond her family, Katniss uses her own life as a weapon against her biggest enemy.

Peeta selflessly wants Katniss to kill him so she can survive the Hunger Games; Katniss refuses.

Katniss's heroism is unprecedented in the history of Hunger Games. She saved not only herself but Peeta as well. Like many archetypal heroes, Katniss still hesitates to accept the burden of heroism. Even on

Conclusion
The last paragraph in the critique is the author's conclusion. The author partially restates the thesis, now backed up by the supporting arguments.

the way home, she attempts to return to her old life. Removing all her makeup and braiding her hair, she tries to change "back into myself. Katniss Everdeen. A girl who lives in the Seam."[4] She wants to return to life before the Hunger Games. Katniss may have acted only to save Peeta and avenge Rue, but with her act of defiance, she has inspired the oppressed citizens across Panem. President Snow quickly recognizes the significance of what Katniss has done. Her heroic actions have caught the attention of the entire country and set changes in motion. Katniss's heroism is now larger than herself and her family.

Thinking Critically about *The Hunger Games*

Now it is your turn to assess the critique. Consider these questions:

1. The thesis asserts that Katniss evolves from having heroic qualities that support only her family to becoming a hero for all of Panem. Do you agree? Why or why not?

2. Do the author's supporting arguments support this thesis? Why or why not?

3. Do you agree with the conclusion? Has Katniss changed into a hero? What details from the text support your opinion?

Other Approaches

The essay you just read is one possible way to apply archetypal criticism to *The Hunger Games*. But there are many other ways you could apply this type of criticism. Analyzing a work using archetypal criticism studies the mythic, metaphoric, or symbolic qualities of pieces of the story. Another archetypal approach could examine the connection between Katniss's heroic journey and the ancient Greek myth of Theseus. A second approach might explore Collins's use of symbols in the story.

Katniss as Theseus

Collins credits the Greek myth of Theseus and the Minotaur as a supporting story when she was developing *The Hunger Games*. A long time ago, according to myth, the city of Athens was attacked by King Minos. To stop Minos's attack, the people of Athens promise to send seven boys and seven girls to Crete every year to be eaten by a monster called the Minotaur. Theseus, a young Athenian prince, decides to end the barbaric ritual. This ritual is strikingly similar to the Hunger Games competition that takes place each year in Panem. A critique could use these similarities to specifically compare the heroic journeys of Katniss and Theseus.

In an essay comparing the two heroic journeys, the thesis might read: In *The Hunger Games*, the heroic journey of Katniss mirrors the heroic journey of Theseus.

Symbolism in Nature

Some futuristic writers create unrecognizable worlds, with elements readers cannot even imagine, things not found in the world today. But the symbols Collins used in the futuristic world of *The Hunger Games* are deeply rooted in nature. These symbols are like those found in many fables. The woods symbolize solace for Katniss, the one place she can be herself. The lake is where she remembers her father. Katniss is also transformed into "the girl who was on fire."[5] Any one of the symbols Collins used to heighten the meaning in *The Hunger Games* could be analyzed archetypally.

An example of a thesis focusing on the symbolism of fire might be: The destructive and the life-giving powers of the element of fire symbolize Katniss's heroic transformation in *The Hunger Games*.

After surviving the Hunger Games, Katniss has a hard time adjusting to life back in District 12.

5

An Overview of
Catching Fire

The second book in the Hunger Games trilogy opens a few months after Katniss has returned from the Hunger Games. Life has changed for her since she survived the games. As a victor, she now receives a generous monthly allowance of food and money. She and her mother and sister live in a lavish home in District 12's Victory Village. They live next door to both Peeta Mellark and Haymitch Abernathy, the other district victors.

Part 1: The Spark

Katniss's love of hunting has not changed. Early one morning, she hunts in the woods outside the district boundaries. She cannot stop worrying about the Victory Tour, a district-wide finale to the Hunger Games where the victors, this year her and Peeta, will visit all 12 districts of Panem. When she returns home, Katniss is shocked to find President Snow waiting for her. Her trick with the poison berries at the end of the Hunger Games forced the Gamemakers to accept two victors and made Snow look foolish. He tells Katniss not everyone believed her story about acting out of intense love for Peeta. He knows Gale is not Katniss's cousin, a lie the Capitol made up to explain their close relationship, since she is supposed to be in love with Peeta.

Snow tells Katniss her actions have caused uprisings in some districts. With a promise not to lie to her, Snow tells Katniss if she does not convince audiences she is in love with Peeta, her family and Gale will die. He also tells Katniss he saw her kiss Gale and knows they are more than friends.

On the Victory Tour train, Katniss tells Haymitch, but not Peeta, about Snow's threat. On the first stop, District 11, Katniss thanks the families of the tributes killed in the Hunger Games, including Rue. An older man whistles a song Rue used to whistle, and then the other citizens of District 11 honor Katniss with a silent gesture of farewell. The Capitol is not happy with this

response. As Katniss and Peeta are ushered off stage, Peacekeepers execute the man who whistled.

The Victory Tour is a blur of ceremonies and formal dinners. Katniss works hard to convince

District 12 is in coal mining country in what used to be called the Appalachian Mountains.

everyone she acted out of love for Peeta, not as an act of rebellion toward the Capitol. When the tour reaches the Capitol, Peeta publicly proposes marriage to Katniss. She accepts, pretending to be thrilled. Snow offers to throw the wedding in the Capitol, but Katniss senses he is displeased.

Back in District 12, during a party at the mayor's house, Katniss sees a secret news report that District 8 is uprising. She begs Gale to run away with her and their families, but Gale vows to stay and fight. Later, she begs Peeta too, but before he can answer, a noise sends them racing to the town center. Gale was caught hunting illegally and has been severely beaten by the district's new Head Peacekeeper, Thread. He vows to execute Gale if he is caught hunting again. At home, as her mother treats Gale's wounds, Katniss decides she will not run away but will stay to help the rebellion.

Part II: The Quell

As Gale heals, Katniss goes into the woods to hunt. While there, she encounters two escapees from District 8. They carry the symbol of the mockingjay Katniss wore during the Hunger Games and believe Katniss is part of the revolution.

The women are headed to District 13, the district supposedly destroyed by the Capitol 75 years ago. The women have heard rumors that District 13 still exists. Katniss sends them on their way and tries to return home, but with security tightened, the long-dead electric fence surrounding District 12 is fully charged. She scales a tree to leap over the fence and limps home, where two Peacekeepers are waiting to question her. Katniss soon learns other districts are also in rebellion.

Several months later, the Capitol makes an announcement. Every 25 years, the Capitol does something special to commemorate the anniversary of the first Hunger Games. The Hunger Games in these years are known as the Quarter Quells. This year, for the seventy-fifth Hunger Games, tributes will be pulled from all Panem Hunger Games victors from the last 75 years. Katniss is the only female victor from District 12, so she is automatically chosen. Peeta volunteers for Haymitch when his name is drawn. Katniss and Peeta will return to the arena. Haymitch and Katniss resolve to keep Peeta alive at all costs. Haymitch insists she form alliances with other tributes, so Katniss joins Wiress and Beetee. They are tributes from District 3, who

Cinna designs costumes that help Katniss stand out from the other tributes—and catch the attention of the Capitol.

teach her how to spot the force field in the training area that protects the Gamekeepers. All force fields have a small visible patch in what would otherwise appear to be empty space.

On the night of the opening ceremony, President Snow orders Katniss to wear a silk wedding dress. But Cinna, Katniss's stylist from the previous

Hunger Games, has added a design element. As Katniss twirls for the camera, the gown burns. The white silk changes into coal-dark feathers, similar to a mockingjay's. After this performance, Peeta lies to the audience, claiming he and Katniss are already married and she is pregnant. The viewers seem horrified the Capitol would force a pregnant woman to compete in the Hunger Games. The next morning, the last thing Katniss sees before entering the games is Cinna being beaten by Peacekeepers. Screaming and shaken, she is launched into an arena filled with water.

Part III: The Enemy

Katniss swims to the Cornucopia and, remembering Haymitch's order, allies with Finnick O'Dair, a victor from District 4 who is a friend of Haymitch's. Finnick kills a tribute attacking Katniss, and they join up with Peeta. The group rushes into a jungle where Katniss remembers Wiress and Beetee's information and spots a force field. She realizes the force field surrounds the entire arena. Before she can warn the group, Peeta walks into it and is flung back, unconscious.

Katniss believes Peeta is dead and starts sobbing uncontrollably, until Finnick tilts Peeta's head back and breathes into his mouth, reviving him. Finnick blames Katniss's emotional reaction on her pregnancy, and she does not dispute him. The cannon fires. Eight tributes are already dead. A bell tolls 12 times, and a lightning storm erupts on the other side of the arena. When it ends, a deadly fog envelops them, but they escape to a different part of the arena.

The next morning, Beetee, Wiress, and Johanna Mason, a sneaky tribute from District 7, join the group. The group realizes the arena is in the shape of a clock. Every section has a different deadly threat, triggered during the hour it represents. As the tributes rush to stay ahead of the various perils, they encounter new dangers. Eight more tributes are announced dead.

The group comes up with an offensive plan. Beetee develops a long fuse made of explosive wire to kill the tributes not in their group. Katniss and Johanna run through the jungle, uncoiling the wire. Suddenly, Johanna flings Katniss to the ground, cuts into her arm with a knife, and smears her with blood. Katniss believes she has been betrayed by the group. Two tributes pass by Katniss, believing she is dead. When they are gone, Katniss searches for Peeta and finds Beetee. Instead of killing Beetee, who she thinks has deceived her, Katniss shoots an arrow coiled with the explosive wire at the visible patch in the force field. The arena explodes.

A hovercraft comes to scoop up the injured Katniss. She plummets into unconsciousness, certain she will be killed or tortured by the Capitol for her act of resistance. Instead, she wakes in a hospital in District 13, getting proof for the first time it does still exist. Haymitch, Finnick, and the other tributes in Katniss's group were part of a secret plan to break the tributes out of the arena. Even Johanna was in on the plan. When she cut Katniss's arm, she removed a tracking device that would allow the Capitol to find Katniss. She learns the entire country of Panem is in a full-scale rebellion. The Capitol has captured Peeta. Katniss is put under sedation again to heal. When she wakes again, Gale is at her bedside. After assuring her that Prim and her mother are safe, he tells her District 12 has been destroyed.

Throughout *The Hunger Games* and *Catching Fire*, Katniss appears more comfortable fulfilling male gender roles.

6

How to Apply Gender Criticism to *Catching Fire*

No. 2

What Is Gender Criticism?

Gender criticism studies texts to see how behaviors that reflect gender are represented, including behaviors separate from a character's biological sex. In society, many gender roles are defined as male or female. But gender critics challenge the idea that all women share one set of behaviors and all men share another. Author and feminist Judith Butler calls gender "performative" in her book *Gender Trouble*.[1] She believes people's actions and gestures often express socially manufactured behaviors. Behaviors performed on the surface do not necessarily reflect a person's inner core. Butler believes gendered behaviors evolve. People choose behaviors assigned to a certain gender and constantly perform the behaviors through speech and actions.

Gender critics seek to identify recurring gender behaviors in a text and to discover whether they limit characters from reaching their full potential. Gender criticism, which includes feminist and masculinity studies, is a helpful way to understand a fictional character more deeply. It is a way to determine a character's motivation for playing certain roles and displaying specific behaviors.

Applying Gender Criticism to *Catching Fire*

In the Hunger Games series, gender roles are often manipulated to serve a purpose. Internally, Katniss does not seem to embody the characteristics usually associated with a traditional female. However, Katniss's gender is mainly defined as female because of how others perceive her, which, in many cases, is the opposite of how she defines herself. In *Catching Fire*, Katniss is pushed into but resists traditional female roles and, in the process, unwittingly becomes a symbol of the revolution.

In the opening pages of *Catching Fire*, Katniss returns

Thesis Statement

The thesis statement sets up the point of the critique: "In *Catching Fire*, Katniss is pushed into but resists traditional female roles and, in the process, unwittingly becomes a symbol of the revolution." The essay discusses how various forces impose feminine gender roles on Katniss.

to her pre-Hunger Games habits. These relatively masculine actions express her true nature. Katniss feels most herself in a world with no imposed gender roles. The woods, she says, "have always been our place of safety, our place beyond the reach of the Capitol, where we're free to say what we feel, be who we are."[2] The woods are where she uses skills her father taught her. After he died, Katniss took her father's place in providing for her family. She even says at one point, "I got my father's blood."[3] She embraced a masculine role when she chose to shoulder the responsibility of being head of the family. She feels a masculine sense of protection toward her mother and Prim.

In the woods, Katniss had a relationship with Gale that resembled one of male friends. The two were hunting partners and looked after each other's families. Katniss never felt pressured to define the mixed-sex friendship as anything but a close bond between two people. She was not self-conscious that he was a boy and she was a girl. However, after she returns from the first Hunger Games, this

> **Argument One**
>
> The first argument sets up Katniss's comfort with masculine gender roles: "In the opening pages of *Catching Fire*, Katniss returns to her pre-Hunger Games habits. These relatively masculine actions express her true nature."

Katniss and Gale start out as hunting partners and friends, though their relationship shifts in *Catching Fire*.

relationship changes. Gale seems to take a romantic interest in Katniss—a change she is conflicted by. Even Snow recognizes this relationship as something more than just a platonic friendship.

To deflect the rebellious impression Katniss left audiences with at the end of the Hunger Games, Snow foists the role of infatuated woman on Katniss. When Snow unexpectedly visits Katniss's home, he uses gender roles as a threat. He accuses her of using a "love-crazed schoolgirl bit" to appeal to the audience.[4] However, he

> **Argument Two**
>
> The second argument reads: "To deflect the rebellious impression Katniss left audiences with at the end of the Hunger Games, Snow foists the role of infatuated woman on Katniss." To support the thesis, the author discusses why Snow pushes Katniss into a manufactured romance with Peeta.

also thinks some viewers saw her trick with the berries as "an act of defiance, not an act of love."[5] Now he wants her to continue playing the role of a traditional female to convince Panem her rebellious action was an insane move by a woman in love. He threatens to harm her family and Gale if she fails to play this part convincingly.

Snow seems to believe a lovelorn Katniss will be perceived as weak and silly, motivated only by a desire to be with Peeta. A defiant, masculine Katniss, however, could inspire a revolution that would bring down the Capitol. Snow will push her into female gender roles in an attempt to diminish her influence over Panem citizens. Katniss must continue to pretend to be in love with Peeta, and her performance must not only convince audiences, but also Snow himself.

Katniss embraces female gender roles when she pretends to be in love with Peeta, complying with the Panem audience's demand for a romantic connection. During the first Hunger Games, Katniss learned the power of her and Peeta's relationship. When they acted affectionate with one another, the audience rewarded them with gifts. Looking back on the first Hunger Games, Katniss reflects, "I'd played the romance angle for all it was worth."[6]

Snow too recognizes this power. When he threatens Katniss, she asks him, "Why don't you just kill me now?" "Publicly?" Snow responds, "That would only add fuel to the flames."[7] Snow recognizes Katniss's actions have resonated with viewers in Panem, largely through her portrayal of the female gender.

In light of Snow's threat, Katniss attempts to renew the romantic couple act with Peeta.

In *Catching Fire*, Katniss's first public responsibility is the Victory Tour. On the tour, the romance charade continues to resonate with viewers. She must keep up this feminine public image even though it means defying her own nature. Haymitch suggests Katniss will be forced to play Peeta's lover for the rest of her life. When the Victory Tour reaches the Capitol, Peeta proposes to Katniss onstage. Snow offers to throw the wedding in the Capitol. Because it all happens in front of cameras, Katniss pretends to be thrilled.

President Snow continues to impose socially sanctioned feminine gender roles on Katniss, but Katniss begins using these roles to her own advantage. Snow forces Katniss back into the arena. Throughout the training and lead-up to the seventy-fifth Hunger Games, Snow continues to put Katniss in situations in which she must act in a feminine manner. For a televised interview, he orders Katniss to wear a traditional wedding dress. A wedding dress would normally be

> **Argument Four**
>
> The author now shows how Katniss manipulates Snow's imposed gender roles to aid herself. The fourth argument states: "President Snow continues to impose socially sanctioned feminine gender roles on Katniss, but Katniss begins using these roles to her own advantage."

seen as a symbol of femininity. But Cinna, already viewing her as a symbol of rebellion, makes the white fabric change into coal-colored feathers. He turns this symbol of femininity into a symbol of defiance. When Katniss twirls, she becomes the mockingjay.

Even the interviewer falters. Cinna knows that for district viewers the mockingjay has come to symbolize rebellion. Katniss has just made a public display of intent to revolt. Snow's plan to crush Katniss's spirit by overlaying her with a feminine symbol has gone awry. She has turned a wedding dress, a symbol of femininity, into a symbol of rebellion.

The imposition of feminine behavior on Katniss backfires for Snow; it actually gives Katniss more support from the people of Panem. In a tactical strategy of his own, Peeta publically announces he and Katniss are already married and expecting a baby. The announcement makes the Capitol look heartless for sending a pregnant woman and

> **Argument Five**
> The author's fifth and final argument states: "The imposition of feminine behavior on Katniss backfires for Snow; it actually gives Katniss more support from the people of Panem."
> The author shows how this audience support is used to make Katniss a symbol of the rebellion.

her husband into an arena to kill each other. The audience is visibly moved by the announcement. They are sympathetic toward Katniss and Peeta and angry with Snow and the Capitol for creating such a situation.

In the arena, when Peeta lunges into a force field and is almost killed, Katniss is shocked into hysterical crying. When Finnick explains, for the benefit of the audience, "It's just her hormones," Katniss is glad Finnick "played the pregnancy card" on her behalf to remind would-be sponsors of her condition and garner more support for her.[8] The tributes and the rebels recognize the importance of Katniss's support by Panem's citizens. When she wakes up in District 13, she asks rebel Plutarch Heavensbee why they went to all the trouble to save her. "We had to save you because you're the mockingjay, Katniss," Plutarch responds. "While you live, the revolution lives."[9]

In *Catching Fire*, Katniss is pushed from the male gender roles she is most comfortable with to more feminine gender roles. By taking advantage of these imposed gender roles, Katniss becomes a symbol of the rebellion. Although President Snow in particular forces these stereotypical feminine

Conclusion

The final paragraph of the critique acts as the conclusion. It summarizes the essay and partially restates the thesis. The conclusion also introduces a new idea: "Katniss's success is the result of her ability to switch between masculine and feminine gender roles as a situation requires, perhaps illustrating the advantage of having flexibility in gender roles for society."

gender roles upon Katniss, his plan backfires. Katniss's success is the result of her ability to switch between masculine and feminine gender roles as a situation requires, perhaps illustrating the advantage of having flexibility in gender roles for society.

Thinking Critically about *Catching Fire*

Now it is your turn to assess the critique. Consider these questions:

1. The thesis argues it was the imposition of female gender roles on Katniss that allowed her to become a symbol of the revolution. Do you agree or disagree? What examples support your own ideas?

2. The essay claims President Snow hoped to subdue Katniss's power to incite rebellious activity. Do you agree with the reasoning in the essay? How might Snow's tactics have changed if Katniss were a male character?

3. A conclusion should restate the arguments and the thesis. Does this essay's conclusion do a good job of summing up the essay? Why or why not?

Other Approaches

The previous essay is one possible way to apply gender criticism to *Catching Fire*. There are many other ways to approach it. A gender critique can also involve searching for gendered behaviors in secondary or minor characters. Another element that gender critics consider is the sex of the author. Gender critics examine how authors may influence their readers' gender perceptions through literature. They examine ways an author accepts or challenges socially sanctioned gendered behaviors. They also look for ways an author makes assumptions about gender. Following are two alternate approaches. The first approach analyzes Peeta's behaviors. The second explores decisions Suzanne Collins, as a female author, made when writing *Catching Fire*.

A Reversed Fairy Tale

In many fairy tales, a knight in shining armor swoops in to save a princess. In *The Hunger Games*, Katniss, the girl, saves Peeta, the boy, rather than the other way around. Peeta does not stop loving Katniss and does not feel his masculinity is threatened by her actions. In *Catching Fire*, Katniss's deliberate goal is to save Peeta once again. In a subtle way, Peeta embodies traditionally feminine roles.

A thesis for a critique based on this idea might be: *Catching Fire* illustrates a reversal of traditional fairy-tale gender roles in that Peeta is comfortable with his feminine side and Katniss is comfortable with her masculine side. One argument supporting this theory might discuss Peeta's profession. As a baker, he is more skilled in home arts than in survival in nature, where he is slower and clumsier than Katniss.

The Author's Gender

In the past, some female authors have concealed their sex in order to reach broader audiences. They did not want to be judged for being female. When *Catching Fire* was released, male and female readers were equally eager to read the sequel to *The Hunger Games*. The fact that Collins is a woman does not seem to have shaped decisions she made, and does not seem to have defined her audience.

A possible critique thesis for such an idea might be: Collins's own views on gender roles are related to the popularity of the book with readers of both genders.

The mockingjay becomes the symbol of the rebellion.

7

An Overview of
Mockingjay

Mockingjay, the third and final book of The Hunger
Games series, was published in 2010. The story
begins one month after *Catching Fire* ended with
Katniss blowing up the arena. Katniss is taken to
District 13. There she is joined by her mother, Prim,
Gale, and the few other refugees who survived the
bombing of District 12, which occurred shortly after
Katniss blew up the arena. Peeta did not escape with
Katniss and is in the Capitol's custody.

Part I: The Ashes

Katniss hates District 13, a massive underground
complex with rigid rules. She eats rationed food, has
limited freedom, and is supposed to follow a strict
daily schedule. District 13, free from Capitol control
and holding a large store of weapons, is planning a

new rebellion. President Alma Coin wants Katniss to be the face of the rebellion as the Mockingjay, the symbol of the rebellion. Katniss is not interested until she learns Peeta is still alive. From Peeta's televised interview, it is clear he cannot tell the real apart from the unreal. Katniss suspects Peeta is being tortured. She agrees to be the Mockingjay because she believes it is her best chance of saving Peeta. As part of her agreement, she demands that Peeta and the other former tributes are allowed to live safely in District 13 if and when they are rescued. She also demands to be given the right to kill President Snow when the time comes. Coin agrees, but adds her own provision: if Katniss deviates from the rebel mission, her family and friends lose all protection.

Katniss's first obligation as the Mockingjay is to create a television propo, or propaganda advertisement. It fails miserably because Katniss is a poor actress. Haymitch suggests filming her in a real combat zone, District 8, where throngs of wounded from a recent bombing lie in a warehouse turned hospital. Katniss comforts them as cameras roll. As she leaves the area, Capitol planes make a surprise attack, bombing the defenseless hospital. Katniss and Gale fire back, taking out a few hovercrafts.

The rebels use footage from the attack to make a new propo showing a fierce Mockingjay, and its success causes the rebellion to swell. In response, the Capitol broadcasts Peeta on television again. He looks worse and begs Katniss not to trust the rebels. The next time he appears, looking severely beaten, he shouts a warning, "Dead by morning!"[1] Snow ends the broadcast as Peeta cries in pain and blood spatters across the floor.

Part II: The Assault

Peeta's warning means District 13 is under attack. Everyone races to a bunker deep underground. As bombs hit and the lights go out, Katniss realizes Snow will keep using Peeta to break her. The other rebels realize this as well, and they send a volunteer mission to rescue Peeta and the other tributes from the Capitol. The rescue team returns with the other tributes and Peeta, but he immediately tries to kill Katniss. He has been brainwashed, and his memories were distorted to make him believe Katniss is his enemy. Doctors believe Peeta will never recover. Katniss is enraged and asks to be sent to the Capitol to kill Snow. Instead, she is sent to District 2. Once there, the rebels, including Gale, blow up a mountain, killing the Capitol supporters inside. Katniss is horrified by the brutality of the rebels' actions. She begs the Capitol supporters to surrender. As she pleads with them, a Capitol soldier shoots her.

While healing from the injury, Katniss visits Peeta in his cell. He still hates Katniss but says he remembers the bread he gave her when they were children. This is a real memory, not an altered one.

With Peeta recovering, Katniss trains for weeks, determined to join a rebel mission to the Capitol. The Capitol streets are loaded with bombs, traps, and other deadly obstacles, known as pods. The rebels refuse to allow Katniss near these obstacles, but she is allowed to go on the mission. However, she will not be engaging in combat. Her team, including Gale and former tribute Finnick and led by her new bodyguard, Boggs, will act in propos. Katniss secretly plans to break away from the group and kill Snow.

The plans change when the troops reach the Capitol outskirts. Coin sends the still fragile and dangerous Peeta to join the group. Katniss believes this can mean only one thing: Coin wants her dead. Boggs thinks the same thing and is furious with Coin. He warns Katniss to be careful.

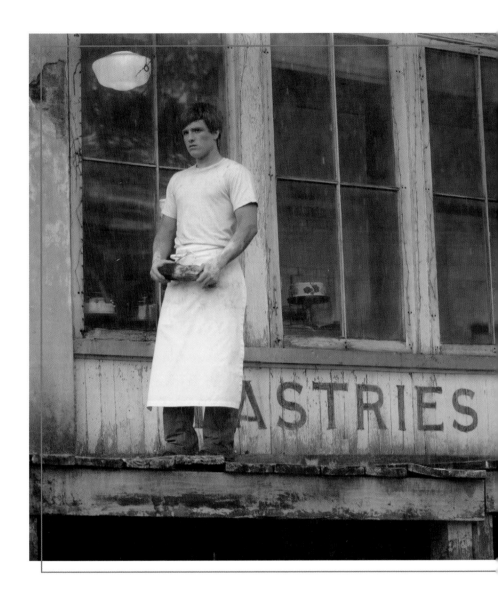

Part III: The Assassin

Katniss's team begins walking down a street to film a propo, but everything goes wrong. Boggs

As his memory returns, Peeta recalls giving Katniss bread.

steps on a bomb, triggering more bombs. Peeta, still delusional, tries to kill Katniss again and has to be restrained by the team. Before he dies, Boggs transfers command to Katniss with orders not to trust the rebels. He seems to know her secret plan to kill Snow and tells her to do what she came to do.

The Capitol has filmed the attack, and the footage is instantly replayed on television. A reporter pronounces the entire group dead. Katniss tries to lead the group to safety, but they trigger deadly pods as they go. Finnick is killed in the escape. The remainder of the group takes shelter in the basement of a shop near Snow's mansion.

Civilians from other districts have come to the Capitol to take refuge from the fighting across Panem and are wandering the streets. Katniss's group makes a plan to split up and storm the Capitol disguised as refugees. When Capitol Peacekeepers capture Gale, Katniss goes on alone. In front of Snow's mansion, children are barricaded in what appears to be a human shield. Katniss watches silver parachutes fall from a Capitol hovercraft. The children reach for the parachutes, believing they are gifts. But they are actually bombs. As the parachutes explode, a team of rebel medics, including Prim, rushes in to save the survivors. More bombs explode, killing many of the medics. Prim is one of the casualties.

This tragedy leaves Katniss wounded and barely able to speak. She drifts in and out of consciousness. When she comes to, she learns Coin is now Panem's president. Katniss lives with her mother in a room in the president's mansion. One day, she stumbles into an indoor rose garden and finds President Snow himself held prisoner in his quarters. He is sorry for Prim's death, he says. But tells her it was Coin, not him, who ordered the exploding parachutes in a grasp for power. Katniss does not believe him at first, but eventually she realizes he is telling the truth. She also realizes that Gale would have known about the attack on the Capitol and was likely involved in creating the weapons used. Katniss is horrified.

On the day of Snow's execution, Coin gathers the remaining Hunger Games survivors. She proposes a final Hunger Games, this time with tributes chosen from the Capitol. Coin forces the victors to vote on this proposal. Peeta votes no. Katniss votes yes and breaks the tie. The Capitol citizens assemble to witness Snow's execution, which Katniss will perform. Coin watches from a balcony. Katniss aims her bow at Snow, then whips around and shoots her arrow at Coin. Guards haul her to a prison cell.

Katniss spends weeks in captivity, heavily drugged and on the brink of insanity. She loses all sense of time. One day, Haymitch comes in to tell her she can leave. Snow was killed in the violence after Katniss killed Coin. A new rebel leader has since been voted president. Katniss was on trial, but a doctor convinced a jury she was a "shell-shocked lunatic."[2] She has been sentenced to live in the ruins of District 12.

Katniss, Haymitch, and Peeta return to District 12. Gale takes a government job in District 2, and he and Katniss do not stay in touch. Katniss goes through a deep period of mourning for her sister, but eventually her life seems to return to normal. She takes up hunting again, and she and Peeta create a book of memories, recording everything they know about all the tributes.

In the epilogue of *Mockingjay*, many years later, Katniss and Peeta have made a home in District 12 and are raising their two children. The arena ruins have been destroyed and memorials have been built.

Gale remains loyal to the rebellion and ends up in a government job. The weapons he helped design were used in the attack that killed Prim, and Katniss cannot forgive him.

There are no more Hunger Games, but Katniss still suffers from nightmares about her time in the arena.

Many elements of Collins's life are reflected throughout the Hunger Games series.

How to Apply Biographical Criticism to *Mockingjay*

No.2

What Is Biographical Criticism?

A biographical critique looks at the personal history of an author and then examines possible ways in which that history is reflected in the author's writings. A biographical critic often considers personal and social factors that might inform a writer's work, such as age, race, gender, family, education, or economic status. A biographical critic might also consider the historical events surrounding the time in which the author lived and wrote. Applying aspects of an author's biography to a text can shed light on its plot, characters, or setting— literary elements that may have been influenced by real events. In its basic form, biographical criticism can be a useful tool for interpreting or offering new points of view about a text.

Applying Biographical Criticism to *Mockingjay*

To create her main character in *Mockingjay*, Katniss Everdeen, Collins used events from her personal life. To create Panem, she applied her understanding of her own social time. Then, she magnified and intensified those biographical elements to design a very real war story. Having been raised in a military family, Collins was uniquely prepared to write about war. Her father's role in the military influenced Collins's decision to write about war, and because of her first-hand perspective, the work is authentic.

Collins based the war themes in *Mockingjay* on her own childhood experience with the military and the way it shaped her thinking. Her father, Michael, was a career Air Force member and a military specialist. Michael's father, Collins's grandfather, fought in World War I (1914–1918), and

---

Thesis Statement

In the first paragraph, the author presents the thesis statement: "Her father's role in the military influenced Collins's decision to write about war, and because of her first-hand perspective, the work is authentic." The author spends the rest of the critique supporting this thesis with comparisons between Collins's life and the text.

Argument One

The author begins by discussing Collins's father, Michael, and the impact his career in the Air Force had on Collins. The first argument states: "Collins based the war themes in *Mockingjay* on her own childhood experience with the military and the way it shaped her thinking."

Michael's brother, Collins's uncle, fought in World
War II (1939 –1945). War was an integral part of the
Collins family makeup. Being in the military meant
the family moved wherever Michael was stationed.
Wherever they lived, Michael made a great effort to
educate his children about war. Collins said:

> *It wasn't enough to visit a battlefield. . . .*
> *We needed to know why the battle occurred,*
> *how it played out, and the consequences.*
> *Fortunately, [my father] had a gift for*
> *presenting history as a fascinating story. He*
> *also seemed to have a good sense of exactly*
> *how much a child could handle, which is*
> *quite a bit.[1]*

Because she was exposed to issues of war when
she was so young, Collins believes teenagers are
ready for war stories sooner than some adults might
believe. Katniss is only 17 years old when she trains
to join the rebel fighters. Despite her youth, Katniss
proves herself to be an excellent fighter and strong
leader. She earns the respect of Boggs, causing him
to transfer his command to her as he is dying. Coin
is threatened by Katniss and sends Peeta to her
team, hoping Peeta will kill her. Instead of toning
down the violence to adapt to a younger audience,

Collins keeps the story authentic to the wars she and her family experienced. Katniss experiences great loss in the fighting, including the deaths of her friends Finnick and Boggs. Katniss also witnesses the death of her sister and is deeply disturbed, to the brink of insanity, by what she has seen.

In making Katniss both a young girl who misses her father and a soldier going off to war, Collins gave Katniss two sides of her own family experience. Collins was six when her father fought in Vietnam for a year. In the novels, Katniss is only 11 when her father is killed in a mining accident. At that young age, a father's absence is traumatic. Collins applied memories of her own trauma when she developed the plot point that required Katniss to lose her father. Collins's own father fought in and survived a dangerous war. In *Mockingjay*, Katniss goes to a real war, not a staged arena. When she patrols the streets in the Capitol, she behaves in ways Collins's father might have as a soldier. She wears a uniform

> **Argument Two**
>
> The author now discusses comparisons between Katniss and Collins and Collins's father: "In making Katniss both a young girl who misses her father and a soldier going off to war, Collins gave Katniss two sides of her own family experience." The author provides evidence from the text and Collins's biography to support this argument.

and carries a gun. She works with a team and gets radio communications. Katniss's battlefield may be loaded with futuristic pods, but she could as easily have been on a war mission in Vietnam, similar to Collins's father.

Collins's father, Michael, was among the many US soldiers who fought in the Vietnam War. His experiences in the war influenced Collins in her writing.

> **Argument Three**
> The author shifts the argument to examine similarities between the role of television in Panem and in the United States when Collins was a child: "The prominent role of television in Panem mirrors the role television played during the Vietnam War."

Collins applies her biography not only to Katniss, but to all of Panem. <u>The prominent role of television in Panem mirrors the role television played during the Vietnam War.</u> When Collins was young, television was very new. Its rapid growth changed people's thinking and altered the collective social imagination. In the late 1960s, the Vietnam War became the first televised war. Some people today call it "a living room war."[2] For the first time, people sat in their homes and watched soldiers in combat running from explosions and burning villages. Some footage showed wounded and dying people. These images of war began to sway public opinion about the war. War no longer seemed like an abstract event in a faraway land. It was real. Not only did Collins see some of these images during the Vietnam War, but she connected them personally to her father. She knew he was fighting in the war she was watching on television.

In *Mockingjay*, Collins infused the story line with television's ability to blur the lines between

reality and fiction. Katniss stars in propaganda broadcasts used as political weapons to control or conceal the truth. When they believe Katniss to be dead, the Capitol is quick to broadcast footage of her death, believing it will dishearten the rebels. Because the characters in *Mockingjay* are bombarded with televised images with specific agendas, the line between what is real and what is not blurs in their minds. For Peeta, the lines between the real and unreal have blurred beyond his control.

The heavy amount of television coverage on the Vietnam War allowed viewers to watch footage from the war in their own homes. As a result, many people had strong opinions about the war, and many Americans actively protested the conflict.

Argument Four

The author's fourth and final argument states: "Both Katniss and Peeta suffer from a condition similar to PTSD, a condition Collins experienced through her father's postwar anxieties and nightmares." The author will support her thesis by comparing Michael's PTSD-like symptoms with those of the characters of *Mockingjay*.

Both Katniss and Peeta suffer from a condition similar to PTSD, a condition Collins experienced through her father's postwar anxieties and nightmares. All the victors, including Finnick, Haymitch, and Johanna Mason, suffer symptoms of PTSD. The violence of their war experiences appears in painful flashbacks and nightmares. Katniss and Peeta suffer from PTSD-like symptoms long after the fighting has ended. In the epilogue, Katniss says, "There are still moments when [Peeta] hangs on to the back of a chair until the flashbacks are over. I wake up screaming from nightmares of mutts and lost children."[3] Michael also suffered from anxiety and nightmares for the rest of his life after returning from Vietnam. Screams from his nightmares used to wake the Collins household.

Collins saw the terror her father suffered due to what he experienced in the war. Yet she also saw it did not break him. He went on to have a career in the Air Force. Like Michael, Katniss also

The stress of battle can linger in the form of PTSD long after soldiers, such as this Vietnam veteran, return home.

succeeds in spite of her traumatic experiences. She plays an important role in overthrowing a corrupt government. Eventually she has a family and lives in relative happiness and peace with Peeta in District 12. Katniss creates a book to remember the Hunger Games and plans to teach her children about the games some day in the same way Michael taught his children about war.

As Collins sent Katniss to war, she applied her own experience with a military father to *Mockingjay*. A steady exposure to information about war from childhood to adulthood shaped her thinking. These experiences allowed Collins to create an accurate portrayal of war for young readers, giving due coverage to the dangers and horrors of combat. If Collins had not applied the experiences from her personal past and her personal understanding about war, she might not have written such a compelling story about the future.

Conclusion

The final paragraph of the essay is the conclusion. It summarizes the essay and partially restates the thesis, now supported by evidence. The author goes on to state a new idea, that by using experiences from her past, Collins was able to write a compelling story about the future.

Thinking Critically about *Mockingjay*

Now it is your turn to assess the critique. Consider these questions:

1. The essay supports Collins's belief that teen readers can handle heavy issues such as war. But some readers have disagreed with her decision, sparking controversy about the Hunger Games series. Do you agree or disagree with Collins's decision to write a series about war for teen readers?

2. One argument asserts that in Katniss, Collins uses her own experience of being the child of a military father. What other examples from the book support this argument? What evidence from the book refutes this argument?

3. Does the essay's thesis give Collins's biography too much credit? Do you agree Collins could not have written the Hunger Games series if she had not had a military upbringing?

Other Approaches

The previous essay is one possible way to apply biographical criticism to *Mockingjay*. There are many other ways to approach it. Analyzing a text using biographical criticism includes examining personal events the author applied deliberately or subconsciously. Collins might have subconsciously applied personal experiences to *Mockingjay*. There may be parallels between her life and Katniss's life that she did not intend. Another alternate essay might examine historical aspects of the 1960s, when Collins was a child, which may have influenced her writing. Yet another approach could explore the connection between Collins's early work in scriptwriting and the Hunger Games series.

The 1960s

The 1960s, the decade in which Collins grew up, was one of turmoil and change in the United States. Many people were angry about the war in Vietnam and were growing increasingly disillusioned and distrustful of the US government. In *Mockingjay*, no government is trustworthy. Both the rebels and the Capitol are power hungry and willing to kill innocents to stay in control. An essay could focus on direct comparisons between people's attitudes toward the US government in the 1960s and the governments reflected in Panem.

A possible thesis for this idea might be: Katniss's distrust of authority figures reflects the disillusionment of many Americans during the 1960s, the decade in which Collins grew up.

Early Work

Collins began her career in television writing scripts for programs geared toward children and young adults. Because of this, she was comfortable writing a fast-paced, dialogue-driven story. She applied this structure to the Hunger Games series, which helped further emphasize the war themes rampant in *Mockingjay*. An essay could focus on comparing the structures of Collins's scripts and novels and the way scriptwriting techniques influence the text of *Mockingjay*.

A thesis based on this concept could be: Based on the expertise she gained early in her writing career, Collins was able to craft an action-packed story that fully captures the chaos of war.

You Critique It

Now that you have learned about different critical theories and how to apply them to literature, are you ready to perform your own critique? You have read that this type of evaluation can help you look at literature in a new way and make you pay attention to certain issues you may not have otherwise recognized. So, why not use one of the critical theories profiled in this book to consider a fresh take on your favorite book?

First, choose a theory and the book you want to analyze. Remember that the theory is a springboard for asking questions about the work.

Next, write a specific question that relates to the theory you have selected. Then you can form your thesis, which should provide the answer to that question. Your thesis is the most important part of your critique and offers an argument about the work based on the tenets, or beliefs, of the theory you are applying. Recall that the thesis statement typically appears at the very end of the introductory paragraph of your essay. It is usually only one sentence long.

After you have written your thesis, find evidence to back it up. Good places to start are in the work itself or in journals or articles that discuss what other people have said about it. Since you are critiquing a book, you may

also want to read about the author's life so you can get
a sense of what factors may have affected the creative
process. This can be especially useful if working within
historical, biographical, or psychological criticism.

Depending on which theory you are applying, you
can often find evidence in the book's language, plot, or
character development. You should also explore parts of
the book that seem to disprove your thesis and create an
argument against them. As you do this, you might want
to address what other critics have written about the book.
Their quotes may help support your claim.

Before you start analyzing a work, think about the
different arguments made in this book. Reflect on how
evidence supporting the thesis was presented. Did you
find that some of the techniques used to back up the
arguments were more convincing than others? Try these
methods as you prove your thesis in your own critique.

When you are finished writing your critique, read it
over carefully. Is your thesis statement understandable?
Do the supporting arguments flow logically, with the
topic of each paragraph clearly stated? Can you add
any information that would present your readers with
a stronger argument in favor of your thesis? Were you
able to use quotes from the book, as well as from other
critics, to enhance your ideas?

Did you see the work in a new light?

Timeline

1962 Suzanne Collins is born in Connecticut

1968 The Collins family moves to Indiana; Collins's father leaves on a tour of duty in the Vietnam War.

1969 Collins's father returns from Vietnam.

1991 Collins begins her career writing for children's television.

1974 The Collins family moves to Brussels, Belgium around this time.

1980 Collins graduates high school from the Alabama School of Fine Arts.

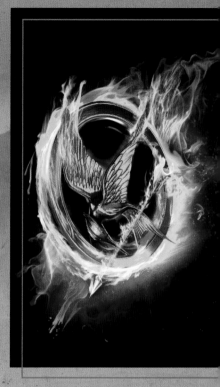

2003 Scholastic releases *Gregor the Overlander*, the first book in the Underland Chronicles series.

2004–2007 Scholastic releases four more Underland Chronicles books.

2008 Scholastic releases *The Hunger Games* in September.

2009 Lionsgate Entertainment acquires movie rights to the Hunger Games in March; in September, Scholastic releases *Catching Fire*.

2010 *Mockingjay* is released on August 24.

2012 The movie version of *The Hunger Games* hits theaters in March.

Glossary

black market
A place where goods are sold illegally.

deluge
A heavy, drenching rain.

deviate
Depart from a course of action.

dystopia
An imagined world that is as bad as it can be, the opposite of utopia.

epiphany
A revelation or an intense realization of a truth.

flashback
A recurring and vivid memory of an intense, traumatic experience.

foists
Forces upon.

infatuated

Having an exaggerated fondness or passion.

motif

A recurring or dominant theme.

platonic

Without romantic attachment.

proactive

Acting with a consideration for future problems.

propaganda

Information intended to damage a reputation or falsely persuade public opinion.

protagonist

The main character in a literary work.

unprecedented

Never before known; an action without previous incident.

Bibliography of Works and Criticism

Important Works

Gregor the Overlander, 2003

Gregor and the Prophecy of Bane, 2004

Gregor and the Curse of the Warmbloods, 2005

Gregor and the Marks of Secret, 2006

Gregor and the Code of Claw, 2007

The Hunger Games, 2008

Catching Fire, 2009

Mockingjay, 2010

Critical Discussions

Bressler, Charles E. *Literary Criticism: An Introduction to Theory and Practice*. 5th ed. Boston: Longman, 2011. Print.

Culler, Jonathan. *Literary Theory: A Very Short Introduction*. 2nd ed. New York: Oxford UP, 2011. Print.

The Girl Who Was on Fire: Your Favorite Authors on Suzanne Collins' Hunger Games Trilogy, Ed. Leah Wilson. Dallas: BenBella Books, 2010. Print.

The Hunger Games and Philosophy: A Critique of Pure Treason. Eds. George A. Dunn and Nicholas Michaud. Hoboken, NJ: Wiley, 2012. Print.

Lynn, Steven. *Texts and Contexts: Writing about Literature with Critical Theory*. 5th ed. New York: Pearson, 2008. Print.

Resources

Selected Bibliography

Blasingame, James. "An Interview with Suzanne Collins." *Journal of Adolescent and Adult Literacy*, 2009. Print.

Dominus, Susan. "Suzanne Collins's War Stories for Kids." *New York Times*, 8 Apr. 2011. Print.

Margolis, Rick. "A Killer Story: An Interview with Suzanne Collins, Author of *The Hunger Games*." School Library Journal, 1 Sept. 2008. Web. 13 Feb. 2012.

Springen, Karen. "This Isn't Child's Play." *Newsweek*. 9 Sept. 2008. Print.

Further Readings

Egan, Kate. *The World of the Hunger Games*. New York: Scholastic, 2012. Print.

Gresh, Lois H. *The Hunger Games Companion: The Unauthorized Guide to the Series*. New York: St. Martin's, 2011. Print.

Seife, Emily. *The Hunger Games Tribute Guide*. New York: Scholastic, 2012. Print.

Web Links

To learn more about critiquing the works of Suzanne Collins, visit ABDO Publishing Company online at **www.abdopublishing.com**. Web sites about the works of Suzanne Collins are featured on our Book Links page. These links are routinely monitored and updated to provide the most current information available.

For More Information

Newseum

555 Pennsylvania Ave., NW, Washington, DC 20001

888-639-7386

www.newseum.org

This museum details the history of news and propaganda over the last 500 years. The museum includes photographs, movies, part of the Berlin Wall, and many other exhibits related to news around the world.

The Vietnam War Memorial

Washington, DC

202-426-6841

www.nps.gov/vive/index.htm

This memorial operated by the National Park Service commemorates the men and women who served in the Vietnam War.

Source Notes

Chapter 1. Introduction to Critiques
None.

Chapter 2. A Closer Look at Suzanne Collins
1. Susan Dominu. "Suzanne Collins's War Stories for Kids." *New York Time Magazine*. New York Times Company, 8 April 2011. Web. 24 Feb. 2012.

2. Suzanne Collins. "A Conversation with Suzanne Collins." *Scholastic*. Scholastic, n.d. PDF file. 25 Feb. 2012.

3. Ibid.

4. Hillel Italie. "How Has 'Hunger Games' Author Suzanne Collins' Life Changed." *Huff Post Books*. TheHuffingtonPost.com, 23 Sept. 2010. Web. 24 Feb. 2012.

5. Suzanne Collins. "A Conversation with Suzanne Collins." *Scholastic*. Scholastic, n.d. PDF file. 25 Feb. 2012.

Chapter 3. An Overview of *The Hunger Games*

1. Suzanne Collins. *The Hunger Games*. New York: Scholastic, 2008. Print. 67.

Chapter 4. How to Apply Archetypal Criticism to *The Hunger Games*

1. Suzanne Collins. *The Hunger Games*. New York: Scholastic, 2008. Print. 36.

2. Ibid. 112.

3. Ibid. 236.

4. Ibid. 370–371.

5. Ibid. 67.

Chapter 5. An Overview of *Catching Fire*

None.

Source Notes Continued

Chapter 6. How to Apply Gender Criticism to *Catching Fire*

1. Butler, Judith. *Gender Trouble: Feminism and the Subversion of Identity.* New York: Routledge, 1990. Print. 177.

2. Suzanne Collins. *Catching Fire.* New York: Scholastic, 2009. Print. 24.

3. Ibid. 322.

4. Ibid. 21.

5. Ibid. 21.

6. Ibid. 51.

7. Ibid. 23.

8. Ibid. 283.

9. Ibid. 386.

Chapter 7. An Overview of *Mockingjay*

1. Suzanne Collins. *Mockingjay.* New York: Scholastic, 2010. Print. 133.

2. Ibid. 378.

Chapter 8. How to Apply Biographical Criticism
to *Mockingjay*

1. Suzanne Collins. "A Conversation with Suzanne Collins." *Scholastic*. Scholastic, n.d. PDF file. 25 Feb. 2012.

2. "Vietnam On Television." *The Museum of Broadcast Communications*. Museum of Broadcast Communications, n.d. Web. 24 Feb. 2012.

3. Suzanne Collins. *Mockingjay*. New York: Scholastic, 2010. Print. 388.

Index

About the Author

Sheila Griffin Llanas lives near Milwaukee, Wisconsin. She holds a Master of Fine Arts from the University of Iowa Writers' Workshop and has authored many nonfiction books for children and teenagers.

Photo Credits